# Crazy Sewing

Hat

Frog Hand Puppet

Mobile Page 60

Chef's Hat and Apron

Pair of Slippers

Christmas Tree Decoration

Playball

Tabard

Cushion with a Pocket Patchwork

Bow

Key to back cover photograph

Snake Hand Puppet Page 87

lion Hand Puppet

Key to front cover photograph

# Crazy Sewing

## Juliet Bawden

*Designed by Jane Laycock*
*Illustrated by Jane Laycock and Shelagh McGee*

Beaver Books

A Beaver Book

Published by Arrow Books Limited
62–65 Chandos Place, London WC2N 4NW

An imprint of Century Hutchinson Limited

London Melbourne Sydney Auckland
Johannesburg and agencies throughout
the world

Beaver edition 1987
Reprinted 1988
Text © Juliet Bawden 1987
Illustrations © Century Hutchinson Ltd 1987

Set in Times
by JH Graphics Ltd, Reading

Printed and bound in Great Britain
by Anchor Brendon Ltd,
Tiptree, Essex

ISBN 0 09 951030 8

# Contents

# Introduction

This book teaches you how to sew, with the help of clear instructions and simple diagrams. You will find all the information you need to learn basic sewing techniques – but the most important thing is: sewing is fun!

There are lots of exciting patterns to follow, but start with something small like the mouse, so that you quickly have something to show for your hard work. Then you can progress to the slightly harder patterns.

The dots at the top of the page show if the pattern is easy to make. One dot means it is very easy, two dots mean it is medium and three dots mean it might be a good idea to get some adult help.

Have lots of fun sewing!

# Learning to Sew

## Tools

You only need a few things to start sewing: needles, thread, dressmakers' pins, scissors and fabric.

It is a good idea to have a workbox to keep all your sewing things in. A biscuit tin or shoe box will do to begin with. If you can afford it, a stacking tool box is very useful, especially for storing different coloured threads. Plastic bags are useful for storing your work and keeping it clean.

Sewing accessories such as threads, elastic, tapes, press studs and buttons are often known as 'notions' or 'haberdashery'. These can be quite expensive, so you can save money by cutting old buttons, hooks and eyes, zips and any other useful bits and pieces off old garments. You can even recycle bits of fabric, especially if you wish to make something in patchwork.

### Some useful tools

A pair of dressmakers' scissors – for cutting out fabric. (Never use these for cutting paper as this will blunt them.)

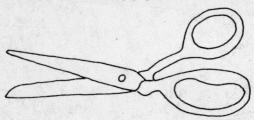

A small pair of scissors – for cutting thread.

Pinking shears – for trimming raw edges. These scissors have serrated edged blades which cut small neat zigzags and will prevent raw edges from fraying.

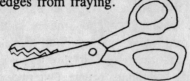

A box of dressmakers' pins – for holding the fabric in position while you sew it.

A magnet – to pick up any pins you may drop.

Thread – for sewing your material. Use cotton for natural fabrics and synthetic for man-made fabrics.

Needles – buy packets which contain an assortment of sizes. You may find that you also need to buy embroidery needles which have a slightly larger hole (eye) for the thread to pass through.

A needle threader – to make threading needles easier.

A tape measure.

Tailors' chalk – used to mark cloth. (It can be washed or brushed off.)

An unpicker – for undoing mistakes.

Needle threader

Tailors' chalk

Unpicker

# Fabrics

## Some basic information and useful hints

You will find that there is a huge range of fabrics available in the shops. Some are woven, some are knitted, and some (like felt) are made of compressed fibres. Make sure that when you use knitted fabrics (like T-shirt or legging material) you sew them with a ballpointed needle. Other needles may cause a ladder.

The edges of your material which do not look as if they have been cut with scissors are the selvedges. If you are using a pattern, you will have to position your pattern pieces in a particular way in relation to the selvedges (see page 17).

Selvedge

When you buy your fabric, you should make sure of various points. Firstly, you should check that the fabric is the correct width (the usual widths are 90cm or 115cm, but these do vary). Then check whether your fabric is machine-washable (some fabrics do tend to shrink or run in a machine). Is it man-made (like nylon), or from a natural fibre (like cotton)? (Man-made fabrics tend to be cheaper, whereas natural fabrics are cooler to wear in hot weather but need a lot of ironing.) Is the surface of the fabric raised (like fur or velvet)? If so, your fabric has what is called 'a nap', and you will have to lay your pattern pieces very carefully so that the lie of the nap is in the same direction on all the pieces.

Although there is much more you could learn about different types of fabric, this is enough information to cover all the sewing ideas in this book.

10

# Hand Sewing

## Threading a needle

**1.** Cut a piece of thread about 45cm long.

**2.** Dampen the end of the thread between your lips and pass the dampened end through the eye by about 7-8cm.

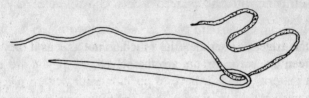

**3.** Make a knot in the end of the thread.

## Before you begin

Before you begin sewing make sure that you are sitting in a comfortable, well lit position. Hold the material in one hand and use the other to make your stitches.

Most people sew from right to left, so it is likely that this will feel comfortable for you.

## Tacking stitch

Tacking stitches are long, level stitches used to hold two pieces of fabric together before you sew them properly. (Tacking can also be used as a guideline to mark where you have to sew.) Bring the needle through to the front of the fabric. Make a long stitch and push the needle through to the back again. Now take a very short stitch and bring the needle through to the front again. Continue in this way until your seam is complete. Don't bother to tie off the ends but leave a long tail instead. To undo, pull the thread out from the knotted end.

## Running stitch

Running stitches are used for sewing two pieces of fabric together. The smaller the stitches and the gaps between them the stronger the seam will be.

**1.** Bring the needle up from the wrong side of the material at the beginning of the stitch line.

**2.** Pull the thread right through until it is stopped by the knotted end.

**3.** A little way along pass the needle back to the wrong side, leave a gap and then pass through to the right side again.

**4.** Continue making stitches and gaps of equal lengths until you reach the end of the seam.

**5.** Keep your stitches small and even and do not pull them or you will gather the material.

**6.** Finish the row with a couple of backstitches (page 13) on the wrong side of the fabric.

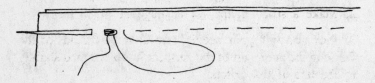

## Backstitch

Backstitching is a line of strong, firm stitches which look like a line of machine-sewn stitches from the front as there are no gaps between them. Several backstitches sewn one on top of another are used to finish off a line of stitching.

**1.** Make one small running stitch then bring your needle through to the front of your material a little further on, at point **A**.

**2.** Push your needle through to the back of your material at point **B** and make another running stitch, bringing your needle through to the front at point **C**.

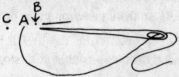

**3.** Continue to the end of the row and finish off with a double backstitch on the wrong side of the material.

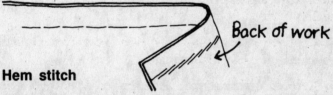

Back of work

## Hem stitch

Hem stitches are used for hemming as they hardly show on the right side of the fabric.

**1.** Tack your hem into position, folding the raw edge under.

**2.** Make a stitch in the folded edge of the hem.

**3.** Pick up, with your needle, two or three threads of the fabric in the main part of the garment just below and slightly to the left of this stitch.

13

**4.** Take the needle through the edge of the hem to make your hem stitch.

**5.** Repeat steps 2 and 3 to the end and finish with a couple of backstitches through the hem.

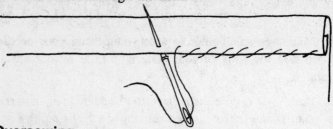

## Oversewing

This is a means of neatening a raw edge.

**1.** Take the thread through from the back of the fabric to the front, then over the raw edge and through from the back again.

**2.** Repeat, being careful not to pull the thread too tight.

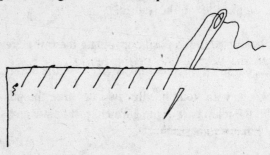

## Blanket stitch

Blanket stitch is worked from left to right, on the edge of the fabric held closest to you.

**1.** Fasten the thread on to the back of the fabric with two backstitches. Insert the needle from front to back, the desired distance in from the edge as shown, then bring the needle down and over the thread.

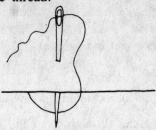

**2.** Pull the thread through to complete the stitch. (Do not pull the thread too tightly.) Put the needle in again, from the front of the fabric to the back, the same distance from the edge as in your first stitch. Bring the needle down over the thread as before.

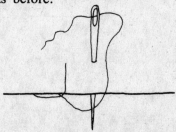

**3.** To finish off, make a short stitch over the loop and fasten to the wrong side of the fabric.

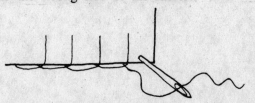

# Using a Sewing Machine

All the things in this book can be made by hand, but if you are lucky enough to have the use of a sewing machine you can work faster. Also, if you wish to progress to using shop-bought patterns, you will find that the result is much neater if your garment has been machine-sewn. Ask an adult to show you how to use your machine. And do persevere — you will soon get the hang of it!

# Using a Pattern

## Home-made patterns

It is always a good idea to follow a pattern when cutting out material. You can make your own out of newspaper for simple shapes such as the tubular skirt (page 109).

**1.** Lay your pattern pieces as close together as possible to avoid wasting material. Always check whether you need to fold your fabric and/or cut two of each piece, or whether you are to cut a single layer of fabric.

**2.** Line up your pieces with the straight grain of the material or at right angles to the selvedge.

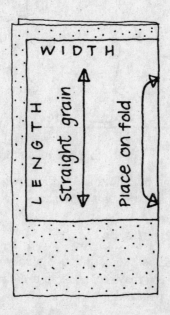

**3.** If your material has a raised surface (a nap) you must lay your pieces so that the nap will fall in the same direction (e.g. downwards on all of them).

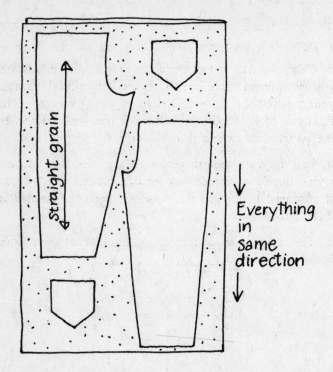

**4.** Pin all your pieces into position before cutting out.

**5.** When cutting out, hold the fabric down with one hand and move the scissors *not* the fabric.

### Shop-bought patterns

When you have had some practice with your own home-made patterns, you may feel ready to make something using a shop-bought pattern.

## Cutting out your pieces

**1.** Before you do anything else, iron all the pattern pieces with a cool iron.

**2.** Check which ones you need to make your particular garment.

**3.** Check whether your material has to be folded, or whether you are cutting a single layer of material. Also check whether your material should be laid right or wrong way up. (The right side of your material is the side that will show when the garment or article is made up.)

**4.** Lay out your pattern pieces. Make sure that you are laying them the correct way up (the pattern will tell you if you need to reverse your pattern pieces before laying them down).

**5.** The principles of cutting out are the same as when using home-made patterns.

# Enlarging a Pattern

Most patterns in magazines and books are scaled down in order to fit them on the page. The pattern is normally drawn on a grid which will tell you how much you need to use to enlarge it or scale it up, in order to use it. You can buy special grid paper for transferring patterns or you can make your own.

For example: on the pattern for the work apron (page 99) one square is equal to 2.5cm. If you are making your own grid paper, you must therefore draw a grid of squares each measuring 2.5cm in diameter.

## Instructions

**1.** Make sure that you have enough paper for the finished pattern. (Use brown wrapping paper or large sheets of newspaper.)

**2.** Draw the squares the size stated in the pattern, starting at the top left hand corner and drawing vertical lines first, then horizontal ones. Use a set square to make sure that they cross at right angles.

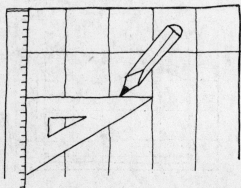

## To transfer the pattern

**1.** Copy the pattern from the original, working on one square at a time.

**2.** First, mark where any lines meet within your square with a dot.

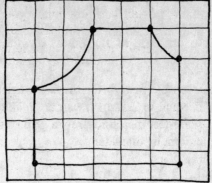

**3.** Then join the dots.

**4.** Copy the pattern into all the squares using the same method.

**5.** Check whether or not you need to add seam allowances. If so, add them around the edge of the pattern before cutting out.

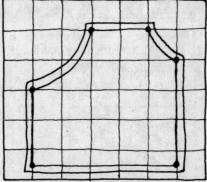

# Marking Fabric

Tailors' tacks are usually used to mark darts, and buttonholes.

**1.** Keep the pattern pinned to the material. Thread a needle and pull the ends so that they are level, you now have a double thread. Bring the thread from the back, through the fabric to one side of the dot. Take the thread back through the other side of the dot leaving a loop of thread on top.

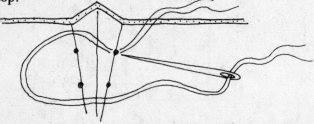

**2.** Cut off the thread leaving a long end.

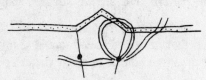

**3.** Mark the other dots in the same way.

**4.** Remove the pattern and pull the two pieces of fabric gently apart. Cut the threads between them. The tufts will mark the dart on the material.

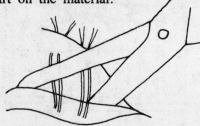

# How to put in a Zip

**1.** Buy a zip 1cm shorter than the opening you wish it to fit into.

**2.** Tack the opening together and press open.

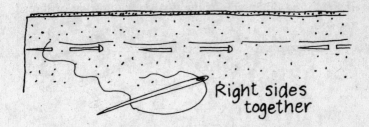

Right sides together

**3.** Place the zip so that it is 1cm from the top of the opening. It should be in the centre with the slide or tab (the piece you pull to open it with) facing the turnings.

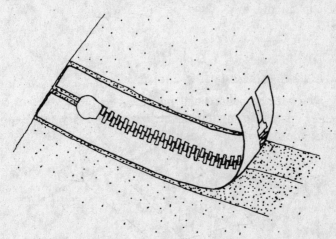

**4.** Pin and then tack into position.

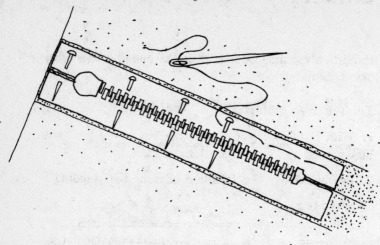

**5.** Turn your fabric over, and either sew in by hand using very small backstitches, or put the zipper foot on your machine and machine it in about 6mm from the centre of the zip all the way round.

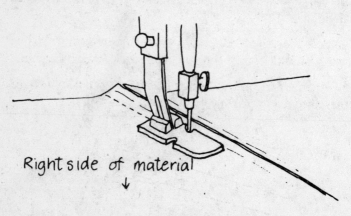

Right side of material
↓

# Binding

Instead of hemming an edge, it can be bound with a special tape to finish it off.

## To use bias binding

**1.** With right sides together, place the raw edge of the bias against the raw edge of the material.

**2.** Pin just above the fold line of your bias binding.

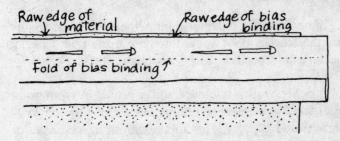

**3.** Tack where the pins are. Remove the pins as you go along.

**4.** Sew the bias binding into position along the fold line using backstitch or a running stitch on a sewing machine.

**5.** At a corner, make a fold of bias binding to take it round the corner.

**6.** Hold the fabric so that the wrong side is towards you.

**7.** Pull the bias binding over so that it covers the raw edge of the fabric, and pin, then tack it into position.

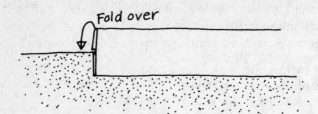

Fold over

**8.** Either hem the binding to the wrong side making sure that the stitches don't show through on the right side, or machine into position using a straight stitch.

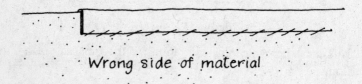

Wrong side of material

# Appliqué

Appliqué is the process of sewing one fabric on to another to make a picture. Before you start, make sure that your fabrics are compatible; that they will wash at the same temperature without shrinking or the colour running.

Your background fabric should be quite firm — a thick cotton or corduroy, for example.

## Hand-sewn appliqué

**1.** Draw your design on to paper first.

**2.** Trace off each section of the design on to a piece of tracing paper, leaving plenty of space between sections. Add 5mm for turning and redraw around each section. These are your pattern pieces.

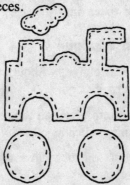

**3.** Cut out each piece of tracing paper pattern and pin on to cloth and cut out.

**4.** Make 3mm snips all round each shape.

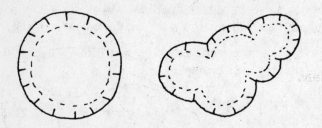

**5.** Turn all the edges under by about 5mm and sew with a running stitch.

**6.** Tack all the pieces on to the background fabric and then hem stitch each piece into place.

## Machine-sewn appliqué

Follow steps 1-3 as above, without adding the extra 5mm around the pattern sections.

**4.** Pin the pieces into place on the background fabric and sew using a running stitch as close to the edge as possible.

**5.** Set the machine on to a close zigzag stitch and sew,

covering the raw edge and the line of running stitches you have just sewn.

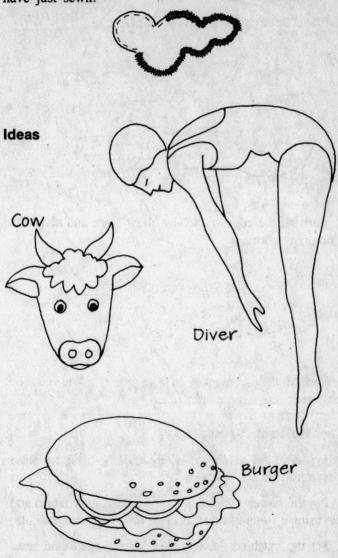

**Ideas**

Cow

Diver

Burger

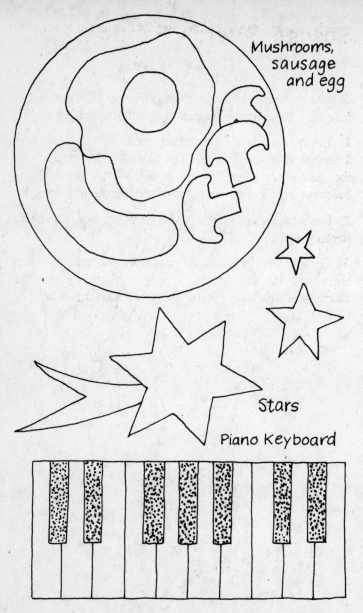

Mushrooms, sausage and egg

Stars

Piano Keyboard

# Sewing Stretch Fabric

Sewing with stretch material is much easier than you might imagine. The simple rules below will explain how.

**1.** Always sew with a ballpoint needle. This is because a normal sewing needle has a point which can cut through the material and make a run or a ladder! (You can buy ballpoint needles for both hand and machine sewing.)

**2.** Use a backstitch to sew seams by hand; this is a strong stretchy stitch.

**3.** To sew stretch fabric by machine, use a fairly short stitch with the machine set at a very slight zigzag. The shorter the stitch the more elastic or stretchy it is.

# Embroidery

Embroidery is a way of decorating fabric using thick thread and interesting stitches. You can do simple things such as embroidering your initials on to a T-shirt or fun things such as a swimmer diving into a pot of marmite.

Embroidery is usually done with Coton a Broder or Pearl cotton and is sewn using a crewel needle. There are hundreds of embroidery stitches, below are a few of the more commonly used ones.

### Straight stitch

Used for sewing dolls' eyelashes.

**1.** Draw a small circle where you want the centre of the doll's eye to be. Draw in eyelashes as shown.

**2.** Thread the needle with embroidery thread and tie a knot in one end.

**3.** Starting from the wrong side of the fabric, at the tip of one eyelash, push the needle through to the right side.

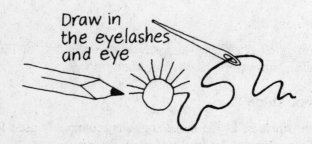

Draw in the eyelashes and eye

**4.** Push the needle in again at the edge of the small circle and make your first stitch.

**5.** Make all the stitches in the same way, working your way round the small circle.

## Cross stitch

Cross stitch is used for old-fashioned samplers and very simple folk embroidery.

**1.** Work a line of diagonal stitches to the right being careful to keep them all the same length.

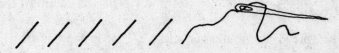

**2.** Work back the other way to finish the crosses.

## Satin stitch

Satin stitch is a filling-in stitch made up of lots of back stitches sewn very closely together.

## Stem stitch

Stem stitch is, as the name suggests, commonly used for making stems when embroidering flowers.

**1.** Make a stitch from left to right and bring the needle up through the material halfway along the stitch.

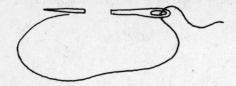

**2.** Make another stitch to the right of the last one, and continue in the same way to the end.

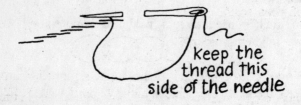

keep the thread this side of the needle

## Chain stitch

**1.** Thread the needle and make a knot in the end of the thread.

**2.** Bring the needle from the back of the fabric through to the front (point **A** in the diagram).

**3.** Push the needle back through the fabric close to the point where it came out (point **B** in the diagram). Pull the thread through, following the needle as usual, but leave a small loop (see diagram). Hold this loop down with the thumb of your free hand.

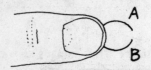

**4.** Make a running stitch forward to bring the needle through to the right side of the fabric just behind the loop as shown. This is your new point **A** and the beginning of your next stitch.

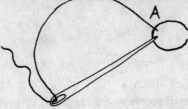

**5.** Continue forming stitches and loops (steps 2–4), to the end of your seam.

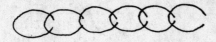

**6.** Finish off by securing the last loop with a small stitch as shown, and make a knot at the back of the fabric.

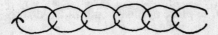

## French knots

These are raised knots which sit on the surface of the fabric.

**1.** Tie a knot in the end of the thread, then bring the thread from the back of the fabric to the front. Wind the thread three times round the needle.

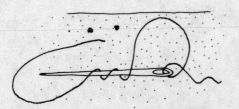

**2.** Push the needle back through the fabric at the same position.

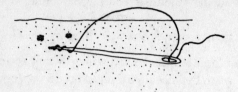

**3.** Pull the thread gently and a knot will form on the surface of the fabric.

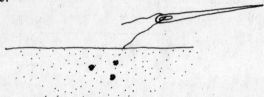

### Ideas

Your favourite piece of music embroidered across a pocket.

An animal peeping out of a pocket.

Your initials on anything.

'Home sweet home' sampler for a family present. The best background fabric for this is an even-weave linen.

# Patchwork

Patchwork is a wonderful way of using up bits of fabric.

If you are going to make something which is going to get a lot of wear and need washing, choose washable fabrics.

**1.** Draw an accurate hexagon, diamond, rectangle (or whatever shape you wish to make) on to card.

**2.** Cut out the shape carefully to make the template (pattern).

**3.** Draw round the template on to paper several times and cut out these paper shapes.

**4.** Place the template on to the wrong side of the fabric scrap and draw round it in tailors' chalk. Cut out the fabric adding a 1cm turning allowance.

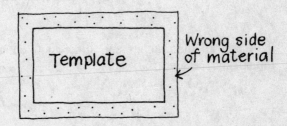

**5.** Place the fabric shape wrong side upwards and place a paper shape into the centre. Fold the turning allowance over and pin and stitch down using large tacking stitches.

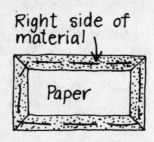

Right side of material

Paper

**6.** Prepare several patches in this way and join together by oversewing.

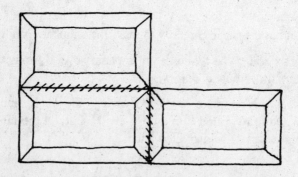

**7.** When all the patches are joined pull out the tacking thread and remove the paper.

# Little Things from Bits and Pieces

## ● Play Ball

This is an ideal present for babies or toddlers, and is made simply from twelve pentagons.

### You will need

Scraps of felt
Stuffing (old tights will do — make sure you do not use inflammable materials)
Needle and cotton
Pins
Scissors
Tracing paper and pencil

### Instructions

1. Trace the pattern on to tracing paper, and use to cut twelve pentagons (five sided figures as in the pattern), from scraps of felt.

**2.** Oversew two pieces together along one side.

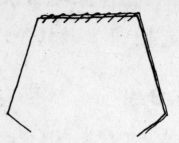

**3.** Oversew the other four pieces around the remaining sides of one of the pentagons sewn in step 2.

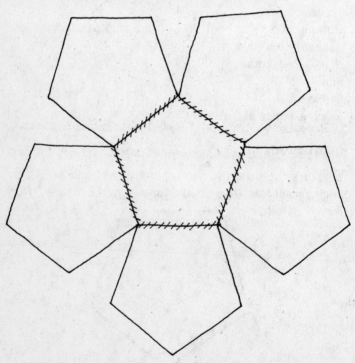

**4.** Oversew the sides of all the pieces to form a bowl shape.

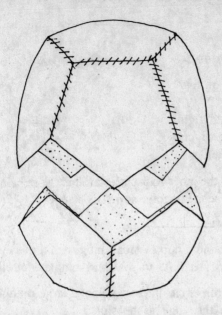

**5.** Repeat steps 2, 3, and 4 with the remaining pentagons.

**6.** Fit the two bowls together and sew up all but the last seam.

**7.** Stuff the ball which you have made.

**8.** Close the last seam by oversewing.

# ● Ladybird Brooch

## You will need

Oddments of felt
Safety pin
Stuffing (old tights will do)
Small mug or cup
Tailors' chalk
Scissors
Needle and cotton

## Instructions

**1.** Draw round a cup or small mug with a piece of tailors' chalk on to red felt, to make a complete circle.

**2.** Cut out the circle and sew a line of large running stitches as close to the edge as possible.

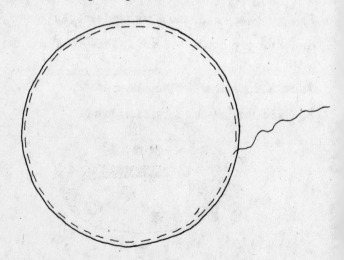

**3.** Gather up the running stitches and put some stuffing in the centre of the felt.

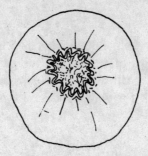

**4.** Pull the stitches up tight and tie off the ends.

**5.** Push the felt into a long oval shape. Oversew the gap to close it.

**6.** Cut the ladybird markings out of black felt and sew into position as in the illustration.

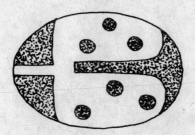

**7.** Sew the safety pin to the back of the ladybird to make the brooch.

## Ideas

To make a bee brooch, follow steps 1–5 using black felt. Then cut thin strips of yellow felt for markings and sew into place. Make small black lace loops and sew into the centre of the back for wings and sew a pin to the back.

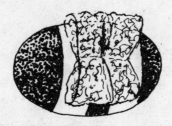

To make a butterfly brooch, follow steps 1–5 using purple felt. Then cut a strip of sequin waste and a strip of glittery fabric 10×5cm. Gather them together at their centres and sew into place. Sew a pin to the back to finish off.

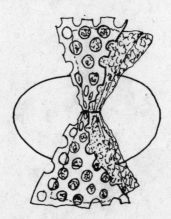

# ● Toy Mouse

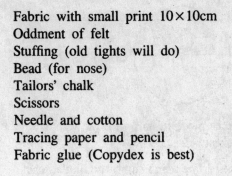

## You will need

Fabric with small print 10×10cm
Oddment of felt
Stuffing (old tights will do)
Bead (for nose)
Tailors' chalk
Scissors
Needle and cotton
Tracing paper and pencil
Fabric glue (Copydex is best)

## Instructions

**1.** Trace the pattern on to tracing paper and pin to your small-print fabric. Cut one piece.

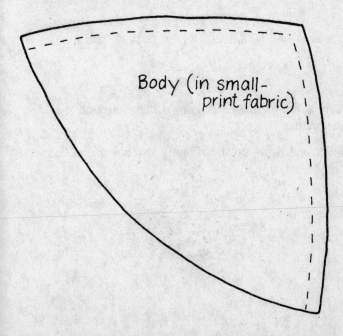

Body (in small-
print fabric)

**2.** Draw twice round a 2p coin with the tailors' chalk on the felt. Cut these circles out. Cut one tail piece in felt.

**3.** Cut one of the felt circles across its diameter, to make a pair of ears.

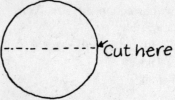

**4.** Fold the main pattern piece in half with the wrong side of the pattern on the outside.

**5.** Stitch down the dotted line using small running stitches.

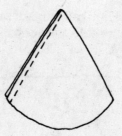

**6.** Sew a line of larger running stitches around the base of the mouse.

**7.** Stuff and draw up the running stitches at the base of the mouse.

**8.** Stick the tail to the remaining felt circle. Stick the circle on to the bottom of the mouse.

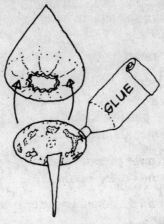

**9.** Fold the semicircles in half to make ears. Oversew along the straight edge. Oversew into position near the tip of the cone-shaped mouse.

Bead to make a nose

**10.** You can finish by sewing a tiny bead at the point to make the nose.

### Ideas
Make a rabbit by the same method but add a fluffy tail and pointed ears.

Sew a safety pin along the seam line and wear as a brooch.

# ● Money Pouch

## You will need

Felt 25×25cm
Hole punch
Scissors or pinking shears
Narrow ribbon 1 metre
Tailors' chalk
Scissors
Needle and cotton

## Instructions

**1.** Draw round a saucer or small plate on to the felt.

**2.** Cut out the felt circle.

**3.** Draw evenly spaced dots around the felt, about 1cm from the edge.

**4.** Either punch holes or snip holes with a pair of scissors where you have marked the dots.

**5.** Thread the ribbon through the holes.

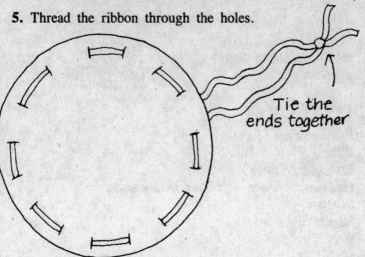

Tie the ends together

**6.** Tie the ends of the ribbon together. Pull up the ribbon to make the money pouch.

## Idea

Fill with chocolate money.

# ● Little Bag

Make to hang from your neck
or for a doll or teddy's
shoulder purse.

## You will need

Fabric strips
Ribbon 75cm
Embroidery thread
Oddments of lace or ribbon to decorate
Scissors
Needle and cotton
Pins

## Instructions

**1.** Cut a piece of fabric twice as wide as it is long.

**2.** Fold the wrong side of the fabric down 1cm and then
1cm again. Sew with a running stitch to neaten.

**3.** Sew lace around this top edge.

**4.** With right sides together fold the fabric in half. Pin then sew around to close all but the top.

**5.** Sew the ribbon by its ends to the top of the little bag.

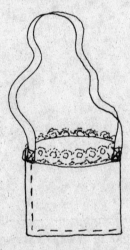

**6.** Turn the right way round.

## Ideas

Make a bigger bag using the same method but sew a pocket to the outside before you sew the sides together. Use cotton tape or thick piping cord for the strap or handle.

Sew a doll or monkey face to the outside of the bag. You can buy these in good haberdashery departments or from craft shops.

Make a long, thin bag to use as a pencil or recorder case.

# ● Egg Cosy

## You will need

Fabric glue (Copydex is best)
Oddments of felt
Scissors
Tracing paper and pencil
Needle and thread

## Instructions

**1.** Trace off the egg cosy pattern.

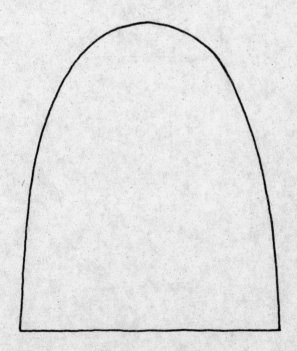

**2.** Cut out two shapes in felt.

**3.** Cut out decorations from oddments of felt, and glue in place.

**4.** With right sides together and 6mm from the edge, sew the front to the back using running stitches.

**5.** Turn the right way out.

# ● ● Christmas Tree Decoration

### You will need

Felt pieces in various
  colours and sizes
Wadding
Ribbon
Beads and sequins
Glue (Copydex is best)
Dressmakers' pins
Scissors
Needle and cotton
Tracing paper and pencil

### Instructions

**1.** Enlarge the Christmas tree design from the grid on page 58 on to tracing paper. (See instructions page 20.)

**2.** Add a 1cm border around the design then cut out the tracing paper pattern.

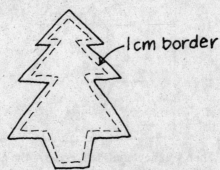

1cm border

**3.** Make a sandwich of two pieces of green felt with wadding in between. Pin the tracing to this.

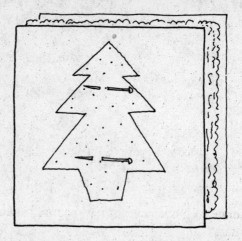

**4.** Sew through the paper, felt and wadding, following the lines of the drawing.

**5.** When you have finished, remove the pins and pull away the tracing paper.

**6.** Using pinking shears, cut around the sewn shape. Do not cut too close to the stitching line — leave about 5mm clear.

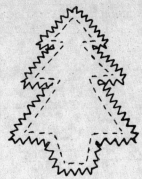

**7.** Decorate with oddments of felt, buttons, bows, sequins, and glitter.

**8.** Sew a loop of ribbon at the top to hang on your own Christmas tree.

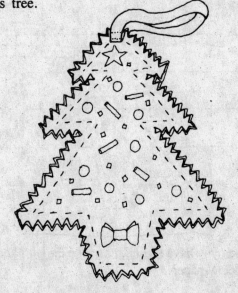

One square=2cm

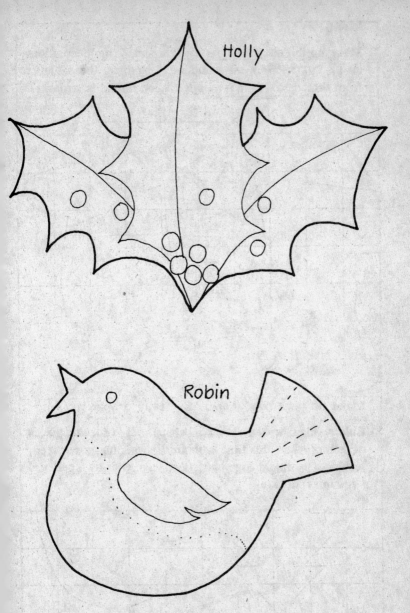

Holly

Robin

59

## Ideas

Make up the other designs for Christmas tree decorations on pages 58–59 in the same way. Or hang these shapes from threads to make a mobile (nylon thread is stronger).

Make up your own shapes. Be really original!

Enlarge the Christmas stocking shape. Sew your two pieces of felt together, this time without the wadding in between, leaving the straight edge open. You have your own personal Christmas stocking.

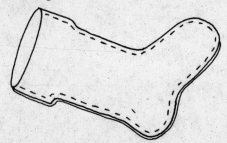

# Bigger Ideas

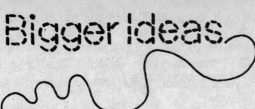

## ● Cushion with a Pocket

### You will need

2 pieces of fabric for the cushion 10×17cm
Fabric for the pocket 13×11cm
Stuffing (old tights will do)
Needle and cotton
Scissors
Pins

### Instructions

**1.** Neaten the top of the pocket by turning one of the 11cm edges under by 5mm and under again by another 5mm. Sew with a running stitch.

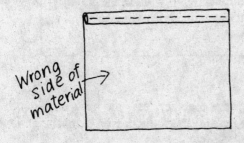

Wrong side of material →

**2.** Turn the other three sides in by 5mm and neaten these with a running stitch.

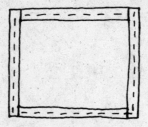

**3.** Sew the pocket on to the centre of one of the pieces of fabric, either by oversewing or machine sewing.

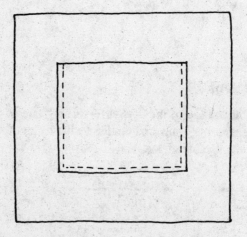

**4.** With right sides together, sew the back of the cushion on to the front, using backstitches or a machine. Leave a gap of about 5cm.

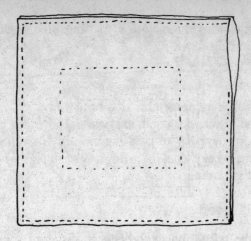

**5.** Turn the right way round and then stuff the cushion.

**6.** Close the gap by oversewing.

## Ideas

Make bigger cushions in the same way using larger pieces of material. You could even try making a big floor cushion for your bedroom.

Appliqué pictures on to the front, before you make up the cushion.

# ● First Present for a Baby

Before you start, remember that babies' toys must be well made and of non-poisonous materials. They must be small enough for the baby to hold but too big to swallow. The first thing a baby does is to investigate things by putting them in its mouth!

## You will need

Closely-woven cotton 40×30cm
Stuffing (old tights will do)
Non-toxic fabric paints or crayons or embroidery silks
Needle and cotton
Pins
Scissors
Tracing paper and pencil

## Instructions

**1.** Trace the pattern from the book, or enlarge (see page 20) if you want to make a bigger doll.

**2.** Fold your fabric in two, pin the pattern in place and cut two doll shapes.

**3.** Draw or embroider your doll's features on to both the pieces of fabric, on the right side of the fabric.

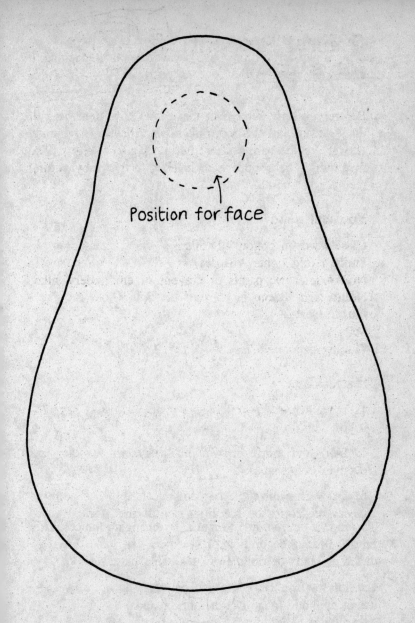

Position for face

**4.** With right sides together, sew the two pieces together, leaving a gap for stuffing. Use backstitches or a machine, and sew as close to the edge as possible.

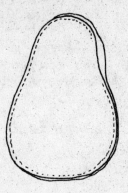

**5.** Turn right side out and stuff the doll. Close the gap by oversewing.

### Ideas

This doll is very simple to make. By changing the colour, fabric, filling, decoration or size you can make lots of different kinds of dolls from the same pattern.

Use lots of bright colours and patterns, decorate by the use of appliqué (page 27) or fabric paints.

# ● ● ● Hedgehog

## You will need

Dark brown, grey or black shaggy-pile fur 21×28cm
Beige, cream or light brown short-pile fur 22×30cm
Oddments of black felt for the eyes and nose
Needle and cotton
Scissors
Pins
Tracing paper and pencil
Fabric glue (Copydex is best)
Stuffing (old tights will do)

## Instructions

1. Enlarge the pattern pieces (see page 68) and cut out.

2. Fold both pieces of material in half, right sides together.

3. Place the pattern pieces on the material as follows.
   **1** on the brown fur
   **2** and **3** on the beige fur. (N.B. **2** should be placed on
   the fold as shown on page 69.)

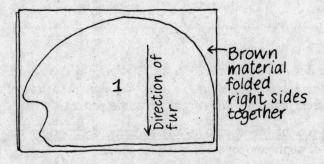

← Brown
material
folded
right sides
together

1

Direction of fur

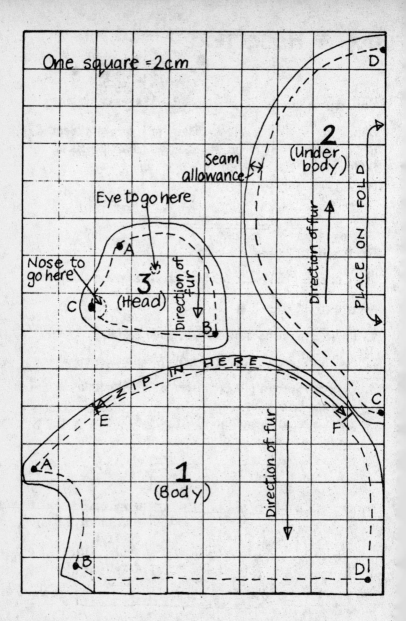

One square = 2cm

2 (Under body)

PLACE ON FOLD

Direction of fur

D

Seam allowance

Eye to go here

3 (Head)

Direction of fur

A

B

Nose to go here

C

ZIP IN HERE

E

F

C

A

1 (Body)

Direction of fur

B

D

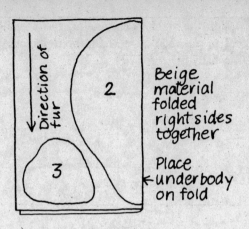

**4.** Pin in place and cut out.

**5.** Cut eyes from black felt and stick into place as shown.

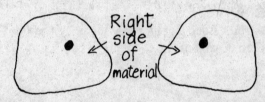

**6.** Pin and then sew the head pieces **3** on to the body pieces **1** with the right sides together matching points **A** and **B** as shown.

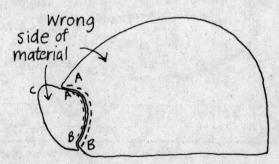

**7.** With the right sides together, sew one head and body piece to one side of the underbody matching points **C** and **D** as shown.

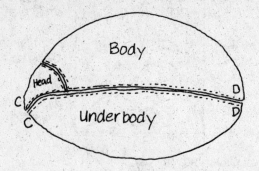

**8.** Repeat step 7 with the other side.

**9.** With right sides together sew the body and head pieces from **C** to **E** and from **F** to **D**.

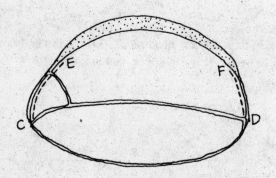

**10.** Cut a nose out of felt and stick or sew in place.

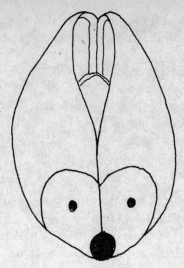

**11.** Fill with stuffing and close the gap **E** to **F** by oversewing.

## Ideas

Make a hedgehog pencil case by sewing a zip from point **E** to **F** using backstitches. (Do not fill the hedgehog with stuffing.)

Make a hedgehog pouch by sewing loops to the underside of your hedgehog and attaching to a belt.

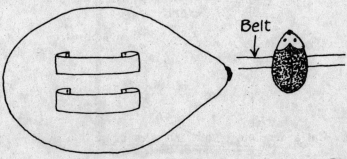

# ●● Play Mat

A useful present for indoors or
outdoors, this is a round
mat with waterproof bottom which can
easily be converted into a bag
by pulling on the cords.

## You will need

Poly cotton 110×112cm (sheeting is a good idea)
Plasticized fabric 110×112cm
Cotton tape or ribbon 160×2cm
Narrow cotton tape or piping cord 375cm

## Instructions

**1.** Fold the plastic mat into quarters and draw a quarter
circle from point **A** to **B**. You can do this by tying a pen
to a piece of string, fixing the string at point **X** so that
the pen falls on point **A**, and then following the curve through
with the pen to point **B**. (If you prefer, you can stick several
pieces of newspaper together and cut a pattern from these
to pin to your plastic.)

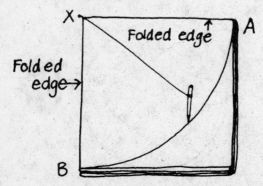

**2.** Cut along the line you have drawn, open out and you have a circle.

**3.** Use this as a pattern for the poly cotton, by placing your circular plastic on top of the poly cotton and drawing round the edge.

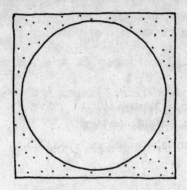

**4.** Cut along the line you have just drawn.

**5.** Cut the wide ribbon or cotton tape into eight pieces of 20cm.

**6.** Fold each piece of tape into half and pin around the edge of the plastic mat at even intervals, so that the loops face inwards.

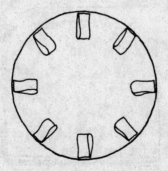

**7.** Using a running stitch sew each piece of tape into place.

**8.** Making sure all the loops still face inwards, pin the poly cotton circle, with the right side down, on top of the plastic mat.

**9.** With a running stitch, sew the plastic circle on to the poly cotton circle, leaving a gap large enough to turn the right way round.

**10.** Turn the mat round the right way, and close the gap by oversewing.

**11.** Sew a line of running stitches around the edge of the mat, about 5mm from the edge.

**12.** Thread your piping cord or narrow cotton tape through the loops.

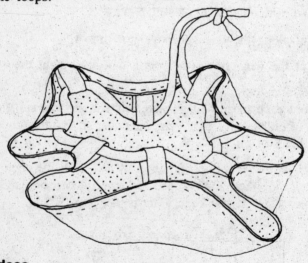

### Ideas

Make a play mat for your younger brother or sister's toys, and a picnic mat for your mum or dad.

# Ribbon Things

Ribbons are lovely for making presents. You can make something that looks very professional for a fraction of what it would cost in the shops.

## ● Bow

The size of the finished bow will depend on the width of the ribbon you use so choose narrow ribbon for a small bow and wide ribbon for a full bow.

### You will need

Ribbon 12.5cm long
Ribbon 5cm long
Needle and thread

### Instructions

**1.** Fold the larger piece of ribbon in half with the right sides together. Sew the two ends together with a running stitch, as close to the edge as possible.

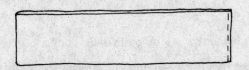

**2.** Fold the smaller piece of ribbon in half with the right sides together. Sew the two ends together with a running stitch, as close to the edge as possible.

**3.** Turn both pieces of ribbon right side out with the seam line in the centre.

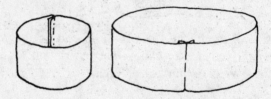

**4.** Slip the 5cm piece of ribbon over the longer piece of ribbon so that both seams are at the back. Secure with a few stitches.

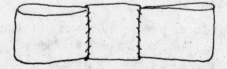

### Ideas

Sew or glue bows on to plain hair combs.

Make shoe bows by sewing or gluing a clip-on earring base to the back of the bow. The flat part will lie against your foot when you clip it on. You can buy clip-on earring bases from most craft shops. You will find that some of them have holes on the curved surface, so that you can sew your bow in place. Otherwise, use glue to secure your bow into position on the curved surface.)

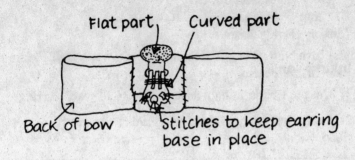

Flat part  Curved part

Back of bow

Stitches to keep earring base in place

Make a bow tie by sewing the bow on to elastic.

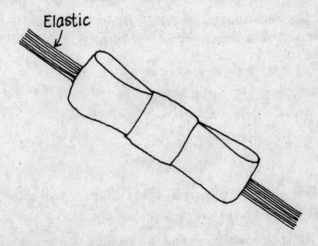

Elastic

Decorate an old cardigan with lots of brightly coloured bows.

# ● Rosette Earrings

## You will need

1.5cm wide ribbon 100cm
OR 2cm wide satin ribbon 100cm
Clip-on earring bases

## Instructions

**1.** Cut the ribbon in half. Use one piece for each earring.

**2.** Sew a line of running stitches along the centre of the ribbon.

**3.** Gather the stitches up evenly and coil the ribbon up. Sew the coil together with a few running stitches.

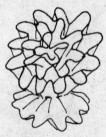

**4.** Sew or glue the ribbon coil on to the front of your clip-on earring base.

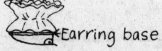

Earring base

# Puppets

## ● Red Indian Finger Puppet

### You will need

Oddments of felt
Adhesive for fabrics (Copydex is best)
Needle and thread
Scissors
Tracing paper and pencil

### Instructions

1. Trace off the pattern.

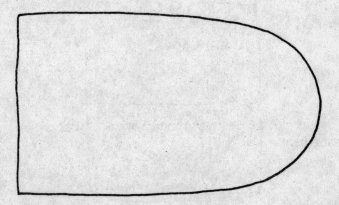

**2.** Pin the pattern on to the felt, and cut out two body shapes.

**3.** Sew the two pieces together using running stitches, leaving a gap at the bottom for your finger. Turn right side out.

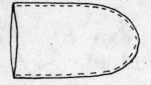

**4.** Cut out features, Red Indian clothes, and an elaborate headdress and glue into place.

## Ideas

Why not use the same pattern and decorate differently for a granny, eskimo or monster finger puppet!

Granny

Monster

Eskimo

# ● Lion Hand Puppet

## You will need

Yellow or orange felt 42×20cm
Oddments of felt for decoration
Scissors
Needle and thread
Tracing paper and pencil
Fabric glue (Copydex is best)

## Instructions

**1.** Trace off the hand puppet shape.

**2.** Place on the fold as shown and cut out two in felt.

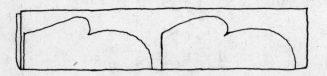

**3.** Cut the lion's features and mane from felt, and glue in place.

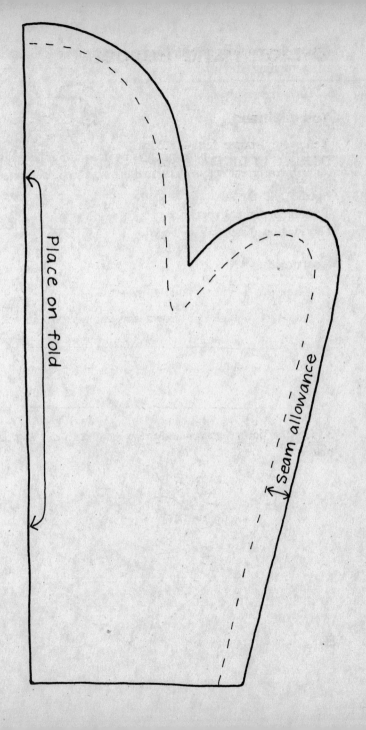

Place on fold

Seam allowance

**4.** Sew the two sides of your hand puppet right sides together using running stitch.

**5.** Turn right side out.

## Ideas

Make lots of different hand puppets by decorating the basic shape in different ways. Try making a clown, a pirate, or a rabbit.

# ●● Frog Hand Puppet

## You will need

Green felt 30×25cm
Felt in a contrasting colour 12×24cm
Oddments of felt in other colours

## Instructions

**1.** Trace the pattern from pages 88–89 and pin the pattern pieces to your felt as follows:

    **1** and **3** on the green felt
    **2** on the contrasting felt

Cut out two of **1**, two of **2** and four of **3**.

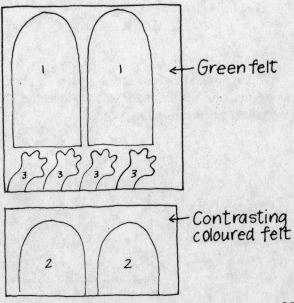

**2.** Pin then sew the two mouth pieces **2** together along their straight edges.

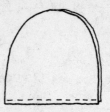

**3.** Sew or glue the features on to the body.

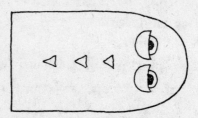

**4.** With right sides together sew the two body pieces together along the side seams to the point where the dotted line is marked on the pattern.

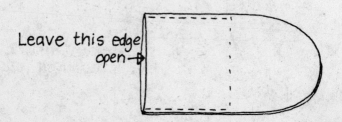

Leave this edge open→

**5.** Fit the mouth piece into the rounded end of the puppet and sew in position.

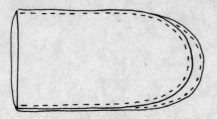

**6.** Turn right side out and oversew the legs in position.

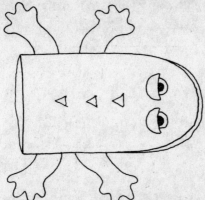

### Ideas

Make a bath mitt frog in the same way using towelling.

Adapt the pattern to make a leopard's paw, a fish or anything else!

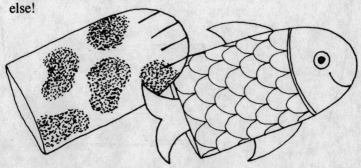

Body

1

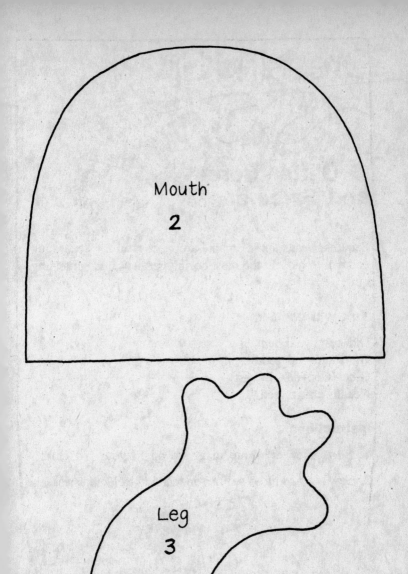

Mouth
2

Leg
3

# Dressing Up

## ● Glitter Beret and Sweater

Sequins, beads and diamanté are wonderful for decorating and can transform the most boring garment into something quite exciting.

### You will need

Old beret and jumper
Diamanté and sequins
Glue (Copydex is best)
Needle and thread

### Instructions

1. Sew, stick or clamp diamanté on to your old beret.

2. Sew star and moon sequins on to a dark-coloured sweater.

# ● Ruff and Cuff

## You will need

Netting or sequin waste,
  or any fine fabric
Ribbon
Sequins, beads, diamanté to decorate

## Instructions

**1.** Cut your fabric to the width and length you require.
The width will depend on whether you want a deep or
a shallow ruff. The length should be three times your neck
or wrist measurement, depending on where you are going
to wear the ruff.

**2.** You can make two different types of ruff, where the
material is gathered at the centre **A**, or where the material
is gathered along the edge **B**. Sew a line of running stitches
down the centre of the material for ruff **A** or down one
edge for ruff **B**. Gather so that the material is the right
length for your ruff.

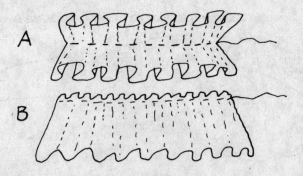

**3.** Backstitch the ruff on to the ribbon along the line of gathering stitches. If you are making ruff **B**, then fold the ribbon over to cover the raw edge and oversew as shown.

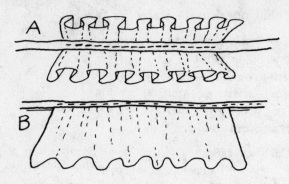

**4.** Decorate with sequins, beads or diamanté.

## Ideas

Wear your ruffs for a special party look.
Use three or four layers of different coloured material for a really special ruff.

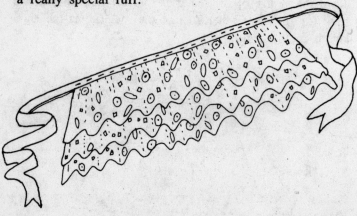

# ● Pair of Wings

Add wings to unlikely places for fun!

## You will need

Brightly coloured material 45×60cm
Needle and cotton
Stuffing (old tights will do)
Tracing paper and pencil
Scissors

## Instructions

**1.** Trace the pattern from page 94.

**2.** Fold your fabric in half and pin the pattern piece in place. Cut out. You will need four of each shape to make a pair of wings.

**3.** With right sides facing, and as close to the edge as possible, sew the two shapes together around the curved edges.

**4.** Turn right way out and fill with stuffing.

**5.** Oversew along the straight edge.

**6.** Sew on to the sides of a hat or headband, or using sticky-backed velcro stick on to your trainers.

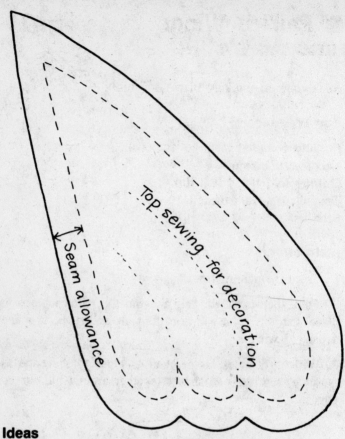

Top sewing - for decoration

Seam allowance

## Ideas

Make a pair of horns instead for a naughty brother or sister. Use the pattern below as a guide.

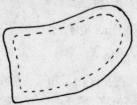

# ●● Chef's Hat and Apron

## You will need

Strong cotton fabric such as gaberdine,
   canvas or sail cloth 130cm
1cm wide bias binding 100cm
Cotton tape or ribbon 168cm
Needle and thread
Tracing paper and pencil
Scissors
Fabric pens
Spray starch

## Instructions
### Hat

**1.** Measure round your head and add 3cm to allow for
fit and seam allowance. Cut a piece of fabric 48cm × the
measurement you have just taken.

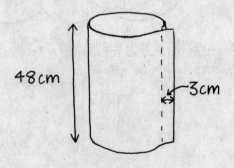

**2.** With right sides together, fold the material in half. Sew the two edges together 1cm from the edge using backstitch or a machine.

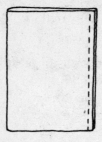

**3.** Press the seam flat.

**4.** Turn one edge of the tube under 0.5cm and press.

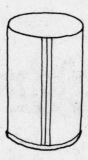

**5.** Measure from the folded edge 10cm and pin, then sew a 10cm hem.

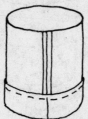

**6.** Sew a line of stitches 2cm from the top of the tube using a long running stitch.

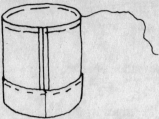

**7.** Gather up the tube tightly. Make sure to secure the ends of the tightened gathering stitches.

**8.** Turn the hat round the right way, turn up the bottom edge 8cm to make a cuff. Spray with spray starch to stiffen.

## Apron

**1.** Enlarge the pattern on to squared paper.

**2.** Out of paper, cut one main apron and one pocket pattern piece.

**3.** Pin the pattern pieces on to your remaining fabric and cut out.

**4.** Turn the edges of the apron under and under again by 1cm, so no raw edges show. Pin then sew using a running stitch.

**5.** Sew the tapes into place as shown.

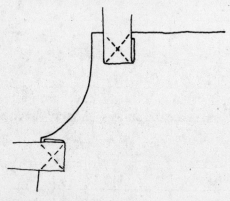

**6.** Turn the raw edges of the pocket under by 0.5cm and neaten using a running stitch.

**7.** Pin the pocket on to the apron and sew into place around three sides, remembering not to sew the top.

**8.** Decorate the apron by drawing or embroidering. Follow the illustrations on page 100 as a guide.

**9.** Remove any pins. Put on your hat and apron and start cooking!

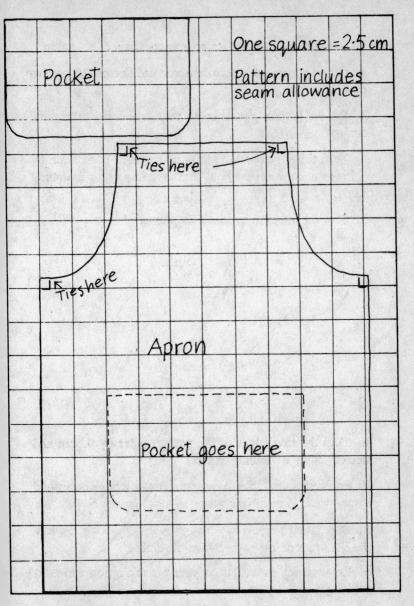

One square = 2.5 cm

Pattern includes
seam allowance

Pocket

Ties here

Ties here

Apron

Pocket goes here

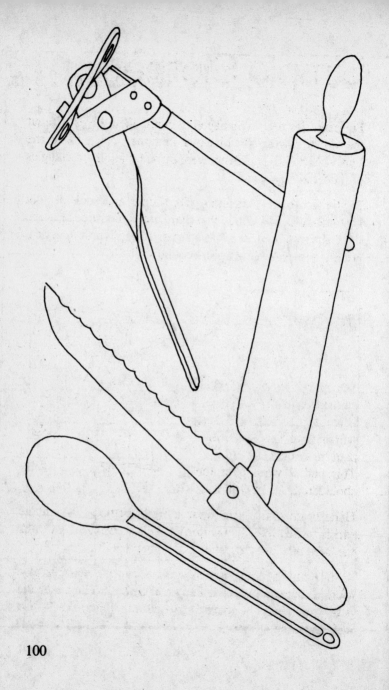

# Simple Clothes

For centuries people managed to clothe themselves without the aid of sewing machines or patterns. You can do the same! Most early garments were made by joining rectangles of material together.

If you go to any museum of costume and look at folk costumes you will notice that there are similarities between the clothes of cultures as far apart as Japan, North America, Africa and many European countries.

## ● Sari

The sari is worn in India, Pakistan and Sri Lanka. Often a piece of sari fabric will have a very beautiful pattern at one end of it. This end is worn over the shoulder.

Underneath a sari you wear a waist petticoat which the sari is tucked into. If you don't have a waist petticoat, tuck the sari into a belt.

A tight fitting blouse which stops above the waist is also worn under a sari. This is known as a choli. You can make your own choli by cutting the bottom off an old T-shirt and hemming the edge.

## You will need

Material 450×125cm

## Instructions

**1.** Put on your choli.

**2.** Put on your belt or waist petticoat.

**3.** Starting at your right, tuck the plain end of the sari into the top of the petticoat or the belt.

**4.** Bring the material all the way around you once, tucking as you go and making sure the sari hangs to just above your ankles.

Old T-shirt with bottom cut off

**5.** Make pleats with about half the fabric you have left

and tuck this at the front, covering the first layer of sari.

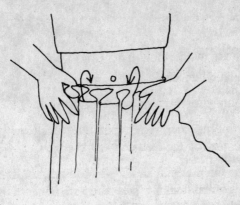

**6.** Take the rest of the sari across your back, under your right arm and over your left shoulder. The highly decorated end of the sari should hang down your back.

**7.** On hot days the hanging end can be used to cover the head.

# ● Cloak

Cloaks are wonderful. You can
wear them instead of coats
or as part of a Batman,
Superman or witch costume.

## You will need

A large square of fabric
Scissors
Ruler
Tailors' chalk
Needle and thread
Ribbon

## Instructions

**1.** Fold the fabric in half and place it against your shoulder.
This will show how long the cloak will be. If it is too
long, cut a strip off the bottom of the fabric, then cut a
strip off one of the sides of the fabric so that you have
a square again.

**2.** Once you have trimmed your fabric to the right size,
fold in half and half again.

**3.** Using tailors' chalk, draw a small curve in the corner
for the neck and a large curve on the outside edges for
the hem. (If you prefer, you can stick several sheets of
newspaper together and make a pattern from these to pin
to the fabric.)

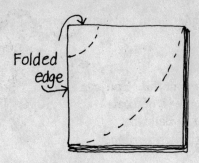

**4.** Cut along these curves.

**5.** Open out the material. You should have a large circle of fabric with a hole in the centre.

**6.** Using a ruler, draw a straight line from the edge to the hole.

**7.** Cut along the line. This is the front of your cloak.

**8.** Neaten the raw edges of the opening and the hem, by

turning them under 5mm and 5mm again and sewing with a running stitch.

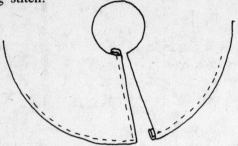

**9.** Neaten the neck in the same way or sew on a collar from any leftover fabric. Sew ties or ribbon at the neck to fasten.

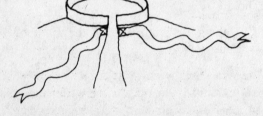

## Ideas

If you are making a witch's cloak, add a line of red ribbon down the edges, and appliqué silver and gold stars and moons all over the cloak. Add a secret pocket on the inside.

# ● Tabard

A tabard is a rectangle of
material with a hole in
the centre for the head, and
ties at the side for fastening.

## You will need

Large piece of fabric
Needle and thread
Pins
Ribbon or tape for tying

## Instructions

**1.** Measure from your shoulder to where you want your
tabard to finish. Double the measurement you have just
taken, this is the amount of fabric you need.

**2.** Fold the fabric in half and cut a hole in the centre large
enough to fit over your head. Neaten all the raw edges
by hemming or binding with bias binding.

**3.** Make sure you leave enough room for your arms to
poke through, then put in a pin, 1cm from either side of
the tabard, to mark where to sew the ties. You may want
more than one tie on either side in which case leave one
pin to mark each tie.

**4.** Open up your tabard and sew on any decorations you
wish such as your name.

**5.** Cut ties of about 20cm long and sew them on to the

tabard where you have marked with pins.

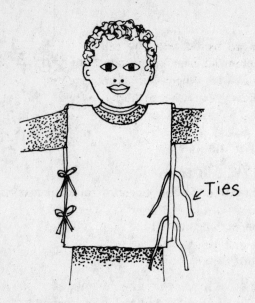

## Ideas

Make a cycling vest from fluorescent plastic.

Make a slightly longer plastic tabard and wear as a painting overall.

Buy some quilting and make yourself an extra-warm tabard for the winter.

# ● Tubular Skirt

Tubes are wonderful. You can wear them all over your body! You can make them into skirts, fingerless gloves, boob tubes, snoods, legwarmers, arm and sweat bands.

## You will need

Stretch fabric (Cotton jersey or tracksuit material is best)
Ballpoint needle and pins
Synthetic thread
Paper and pencil (for pattern)
Scissors
Tape measure
Elastic
Safety pins

## Instructions

**1.** Measure your hips and add 7.5cm to this measurement. This is for ease of movement and to stop you looking like a sausage in a very tight skin. This measurement is how wide you need to cut your fabric. Measure from your waist to where you want the skirt to end (thigh, knee, or calf) and add 5cm for seam allowance. This is the length you need to cut your fabric.

**2.** Now make a pattern. If your paper is too small, stick a few pieces together. Using a pencil and ruler, draw a rectangle, with sides of the correct length and width (as worked out in 1). Cut this out. Write the word WIDTH across the pattern and the word LENGTH down the pattern, to remind you which way to cut the material.

**3.** Using the ballpoint pins, pin the pattern on to the fabric. Make sure that the width stretches rather than the length.

**4.** Cut out one pattern shape.

**5.** Fold the skirt shape in half lengthways, with the right sides together. Pin together with a 1cm seam allowance. Sew down this seam with backstitch if hand sewing or a narrow zigzag if using a sewing machine.

**6.** Make a channel to carry the elastic. Fold over the top of the skirt 1cm, and pin on to the rest of the skirt. Hem, leaving a 2cm gap through which to thread the elastic.

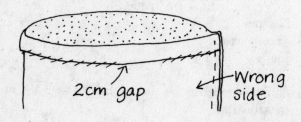

**7.** Safety pin one end of the elastic to the hem next to the 2cm gap. Put a safety pin on the other end of the elastic, and push this through the hem to thread the elastic. Tie the two ends of elastic together and try on the skirt, adjusting the elastic as necessary. Cut off any excess elastic. Undo the knot in the elastic and sew the two ends together, then sew up the hem opening.

**8.** Pin up the bottom of the skirt to make a hem. Try it on to see that it is the correct length and hem.

# ●●● Wrap Around Skirt

## You will need

Fabric
Bias binding
Needle and thread
Scissors

## Instructions

**1.** Measure your waist, add 30cm and double – this is the width of fabric needed. Measure down from your waist to get the length of the skirt. Cut your material to this size.

**2.** Bind two short and one long side (see page 25).

**3.** Sew a line of long running stitches 1.5cm from the unbound edge of the material.

**4.** Put pins along the line of stitches to mark at intervals of a quarter.

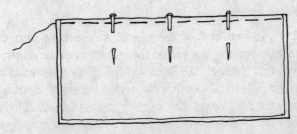

**5.** Cut a waistband 30×5cm. Turn one 30cm edge under by 0.5cm and neaten with running stitches. Mark at quarter intervals along with pins.

**6.** Pull the line of gathering stitches on the skirt, until they measure the same as the waistband.

**7.** With right sides together, pin the skirt on to the raw edge of the waistband, matching the pins at the quarterly intervals.

**8.** With right sides together, tack then sew the skirt on to the waistband.

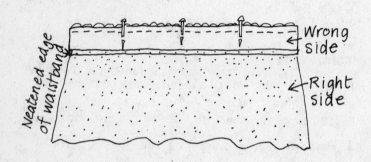

**9.** Fold the waistband over the raw edges of the skirt and sew using a hemming stitch.

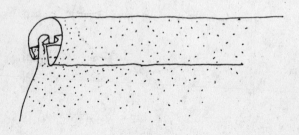

**10.** To make ties, cut 100cm of bias binding in half and then fold down the raw ends and hem.

**11.** Push each tie into the open end of the waistband and sew into position.

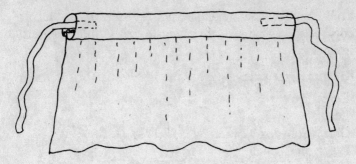

**12.** Wear your skirt by wrapping it round you and tying the ties.

# ●● Pair of Slippers

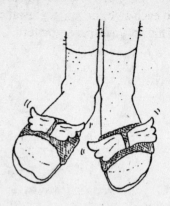

## You will need

Towelling or felt 50cm
Wadding or foam 50cm
Cereal box
Leather
Glue (Copydex is best)
Paper and pencil

## Instructions

**1.** Draw round your feet on to paper, and add 1cm for seam allowance all the way round.

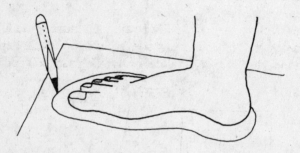

**2.** Mark **R** for right foot and **L** for left foot. Cut out the paper pattern pieces.

**3.** Pin the patterns on to the felt or towelling and cut one **R** and one **L**.

**4.** Cut the 1cm seam allowance off the paper pattern pieces and then, using the rest of the pattern, cut one **R** and one **L** in foam, card and leather.

114

**5.** Cut a strip of paper 20×6cm. Place this over the foot and mark at the sides where it meets the foot. Add 1cm to each side for seam allowance, and cut down to this size. This is your paper pattern.

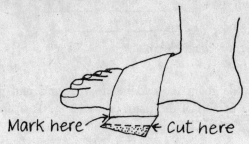

Mark here → ← Cut here

**6.** Cut two pieces of towelling or felt 20×12.5cm. Cut two pieces of foam or wadding, 20×6cm.

**7.** Place one piece of the foam or wadding into the centre of one of the pieces of towelling or felt. Turn under the edges of the towelling or felt so that the foam or wadding is completely hidden and sew with a hemming stitch. Repeat with the other strip of towelling or felt and foam or wadding.

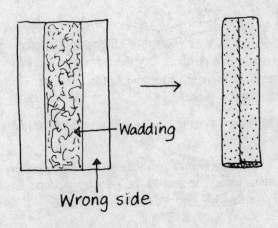

Wadding

Wrong side

**8.** Shape the sides of your towelling or felt strip as in the paper pattern you cut in step 5.

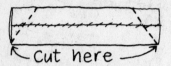

**9.** Glue the foam or wadding to the card and glue the towelling on top of the foam or wadding. Turn the edges under and stick to the back of the card.

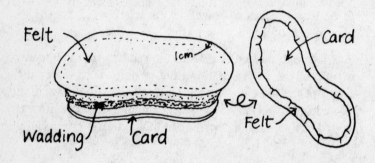

**10.** Pin the felt or towelling strips, so that the seam is underneath, into position. Try the slipper on and adjust to fit.

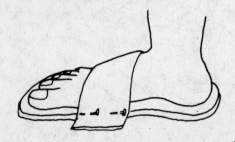

**11.** Turn the edges of the strip under and sew to the underneath of the slipper.

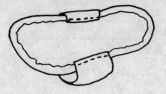

**12.** Glue the leather soles to the bottom of the slippers.

## Ideas

Make animal, wings, or funny face shapes using the method as for the Christmas Decorations (page 55) and sew them into the centres of the slippers.

Or sew on sequins or decorate with bows.

# ●● Baggy Trousers

These trousers are comfortable to wear
and can be made from very fine
or fairly thick material.

## You will need

A pair of your trousers
Fabric
Elastic ribbon or cord
Large safety pin for threading
Tailors' chalk
Needle and thread
Pins
Scissors

## Instructions

**1.** Take a piece of fabric a bit wider than your hip measurement and twice the length from your waist to the ground. Fold in half lengthways.

**2.** Fold your trousers in half as shown. Pin on to the folded material.

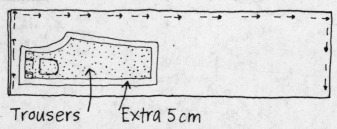

Trousers    Extra 5 cm

**3.** Draw round the shape adding an extra 5cm all the way round.

**4.** Unpin your trousers, and fold the other way as shown. Pin to your material and draw round them again adding an extra 5cm.

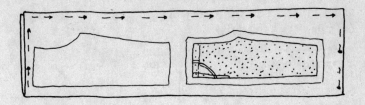

**5.** Cut out the shapes you have just drawn.

**6.** With the right sides together, pin the two back pieces together down the centre back seam and sew 1.5cm from the edge. The back has a larger curve than the front.

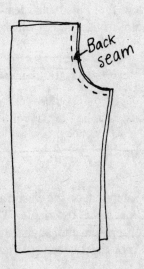

Back seam

**7.** Repeat step 5 with the two front pieces.

**8.** With right sides together, pin the front to the back down the inside and outside legs. Sew 1.5cm from the edge.

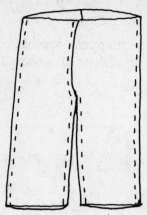

**9.** Fold the top down by 2.5cm to make the waistband.

**10.** Pin then sew the waistband, leaving a gap of about 2.5cm at the centre front, through which to thread the elastic.

**11.** Put a large safety pin on the elastic and thread it through the waistband you have just made. Turn right side out, then try the trousers on and adjust the waistband to fit. Either sew or knot the two ends of the elastic together.

**12.** Turn up and pin the trousers, so they fit. Sew with a running stitch to neaten.

# ● ● Hat

This hat is easy to make and you can achieve many different styles by the addition of appliquéd shapes, feathers or beads.

## You will need

Felt 50cm
Thick interfacing 20cm (buy the thickest that you can)
Lining fabric 20cm
Needle and thread
Paper and pencil

## Instructions

**1.** Draw round a tea plate to make the circular part of the pattern.

**2.** Using the pattern you have just made, cut a circle of each of the following: felt, interfacing and lining fabric.

**3.** With right sides facing outwards, sandwich the interfacing between the felt and the lining fabric and backstitch them together as close to the edge as possible.

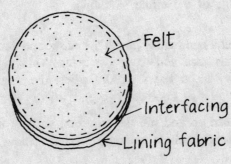

Felt

Interfacing

Lining fabric

**4.** Using a tape measure, measure round the circumference of your circle. Add 2cm for seam allowance.

**5.** Cut a rectangle of felt 18cm wide. The length should be the measurement reached in step 4.

**6.** Pin the rectangle to the edge of the circle as shown with the felt facing inwards. Tack then oversew the rectangle to the circle.

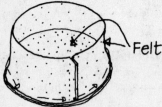

**7.** Sew the two overlapping pieces together to make a seam.

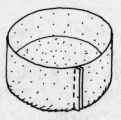

**8.** Fold the 18cm length in half and oversew the edge to the edge of the circle as shown.

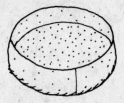

**9.** Turn right way round. Your hat is now finished.

## Ideas

Decorate with felt shapes as in Christmas Decorations (page 55) or add bows, feathers, beads and sequins.

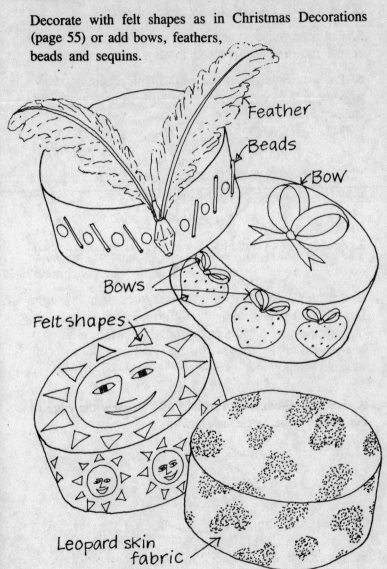

Feather

Beads

Bow

Bows

Felt shapes

Leopard skin fabric

# Cheap and Cheerful

## ● Odd Sock and Glove

Everyone loses the occasional glove or sock. Here are some ideas for using up the remaining partners!

### Cleaning Glove

This zany idea is not as silly as it first appears, as people do like to protect their hands when doing household chores.

Cut out long red nails from felt and stick them on to the fingers of an odd or old cotton glove. Sew a duster to the underside of the fingers, being careful not to sew through both layers of the gloves. For real glamour, add a sequin bracelet to the cuff.

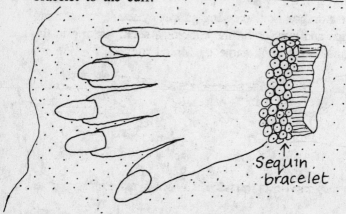

Sequin bracelet

## Puppets

Turn a single glove into a spider, crab or octopus. For a spider sew a black pom-pom (See *Crazy Knitting*) on to the back of the glove. For an octopus sew small buttons all over the fingers of the glove to represent suckers. For a crab, stick bright red claws on to the thumb and forefinger, and small black buttons on the back of the glove for eyes.

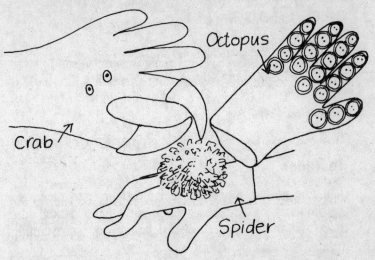

Make a dragon or snake sock puppet by sewing or sticking sequins and buttons on the back of a sock, tucking in the toe and inserting a flame or forked tongue.

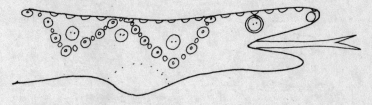

Sew long ears on to the sides of a sock to make a dog puppet.

## Dolls

Knitted fabrics like old socks and mittens are good for making rag doll heads or socks for a doll.

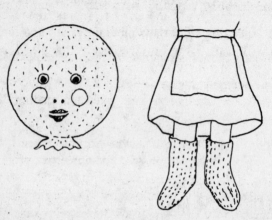

## Stuffing

Cut fine gloves and socks and old tights into pieces for stuffing soft toys. Make sure you really have lost the other one, and that they are washed before you start cutting!

# New from Old

Before throwing anything away see if it can be recycled.

Keep a box or tin for old buttons.

Always cut zips off old clothes as these are expensive to buy.

An old pompom hat can be turned into a tea cosy by cutting holes for the handle and spout and binding the edges to stop them fraying.

Large pieces of material such as curtains, sheets, blankets or old tablecloths can be used for numerous projects. Try making a simple poncho by cutting a hole in the centre of a blanket and embroidering it. Do check that you can use the blanket first though! Make a cloak (page 104) from old and unwanted curtains.

Turn an old pair of jeans into a bag by cutting off the legs, turning them inside out and sewing across the bottom with a backstitch.
Turn the right way out and sew a strap from one side to the other.

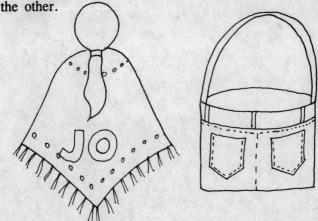

# Acknowledgments

Tootal Crafts for supplying all the sewing threads and notions used throughout this book.

Brother and Jones for the use of the Compal Galexie sewing machine.

Ells and Farrier, London, for supplying sequins beads, and sequin waste.
Mail Order: Ells and Farrier,
Unit 26, Chiltern Trading Estate,
Earl Howe Road, Holmer Green,
High Wycombe, Bucks.

Unibond, Surrey, for supplying Copydex, which was used thoughout the book.